Eternity's Woods

Eternity's Woods

PAUL ZWEIG

Postscript by Galway Kinnell

WESLEYAN UNIVERSITY PRESS
MIDDLETOWN, CONNECTICUT

The following magazines first published the poems listed: *American Poetry Review:* Aunt Lil, the Classroom, The Other Side, Prayer Against Too Much, Early Waking, Eternity's Woods, The Other Ocean, A Fly on the Water, Life Story, The Esplanade (as Father); *Antaeus:* Jacob and the Angel; *Ironwood:* Stanzas in an Emergency; *The New Yorker:* The River, The End Circulates in the Wide Space of Summer, The Taking Away, The Perfect Sleepers; *The Paris Review:* Snow, Wasps, Parting the Sea, The Dance of Death.

All inquiries and permissions requests should be addressed to the Publisher, Wesleyan University Press, 110 Mt. Vernon Street, Middletown, Connecticut 06457.

Distributed by Harper & Row Publishers, Keystone Industrial Park, Scranton, Pennsylvania 18512.

LIBRARY OF CONGRESS CATALOGING IN PUBLICATION DATA
Zweig, Paul.
Eternity's woods.

(Wesleyan poetry)
I. Title. II. Series.
PS3576.W4E88 1985 811'.54 84-20859
ISBN 0-8195-5135-X
ISBN 0-8195-6134-7 PBK

Manufactured in the United States of America

First printing, 1985; second printing, 1985
Wesleyan Paperback, 1985; second printing, 1985

for Baba

Contents

Part One

Aunt Lil

I

They brought her to the hospital
On one of those April days
That remind us we will never live enough.
That the soft smell of leaves, flowering breeze,
The silver light flashing from windows,
Will always be too much for us.

She kicks the covers back, not caring
If we see her enormous thighs, her birthmark
Tufted with secret hairs only lovers had seen.
When her lips won't form around her thought,
She cries out girlishly, "I don't know, I don't know."
Her large eyes roll and stare, as if looking
For someone to pry her from her failing flesh.

II

A beach: scalloped sand, soft rasping waves;
My parents searching frantically to see
If I had drowned, or if, like the fish
In the tale, I could breathe their angry
Guilt and make a life of it.
With a small boy's genius, I imitated childhood,
Taking you, my large-eyed beautiful aunt,
To love passionately and simply.

Cruel and soaring,
You battered those you loved,
As if ecstasy and cruelty were the same.
Yet at times you were happier than anyone;
So drunk on yourself, you could hardly
Walk down stairs for the stumbling heavens at your heels.

III

I remember sitting with you on the subway,
Thick-headed with fever.
You opened your newspaper
To a cloud boiling on a stalk of light,
A single word, Hiroshima.
Amid the screeching of subway metal,
The headlines drooping on front pages, your voice,
Your immense body, seemed to fill the subway car.

I hadn't heard yet of your manic flights,
The electroshock, the family's
Embarrassed hush at your desperate ways.

You were sick of too much:
Hope fucking laughter.
Yet to me you were beautiful,
A brown moon of flesh.
And the boy who lived as in a cold sleep
Came strangely forth into your larger louder life.

IV

Old death,
Will you come with me today
To meet someone I love?
We can walk there along the river
Past tenements of red brick,
And barely thickening April branches:
The river's grey-shine spinning past us,
An orange tugboat,
A low-swimming freighter out toward Jersey.

Will you teach me about her rooms
Filled with a westward light,
Her books thumbed and bright along one wall?
Nowhere the smallest hint of a failed life,
No dust balls of loneliness or fright.

Yesterday I sat on her bed,
Holding her soft old woman's hands.
She forgave me for being young,
For the scared distance I put between us all these years.
Her enormous eyes never looked at me,
Only her hands spoke,
Her fingers stirring so I would know.

Old death,
The more I see you, the more
I know of restless eyes, vulnerable mouths,
Uncertain language of lips.

For I have learned what I came for:
My mad old aunt loved life.
She only hurt us when she was afraid
That it would burst in her.
She never gave in to her old age,
But expelled it from her,
And hung clean sweet living upon her walls.

Snow

Love is all we could manage,
Its particles floating from the hard rim of the air.
Our tracks were clear in the fresh chance
Heaven threw behind us. The pain
Went on searching behind your face,
The snow went on falling.

Once your voice worked so gently into my brain,
It took root in the mind-dark
And branched forth again, singing.

Character may be a failure of love;
This morning, I want to love you,
And the birch trunks invisible on snow,
Your hand pushed warmly into my pocket;
I want to love the darkening blue at the
    sky's edge,
Our thoughts fumbling to hold on;
I want to love our breath-smoke warming
The air, then vanishing
In the frozen February day.

The Classroom

These rows of half-made faces listen
To my friend Sara lecture on Balzac.
Old Goriot stumbles down Rue Neuve Sainte Geneviève,
Into the garden of the Pension Vauquer,
With the jangled gait of his obsession.
"My daughters, my daughters," he calls his lurch
Into nothing; a man without a net, a man
Whom the animal patience of these listening children
Will not keep from hitting bottom.

Sara's worried face, her hands playing nervously
On the bare desk, draw a noose
Of affectionate tension around the class.
She talks of King Lear and his daughters,
Goriot and his daughters, a street winding
Between the stucco'd grimace of houses, shops,
Until that clarity on the narrow bed,
Acrobatic laughter of foot soles gliding over nothing.

I listen to Sara's concentrated voice,
Its tremor of panic, its counter-
Note of joy, even triumph, at saying everything
—All of life, *all of her life*—
In this story about a man who lived
Against reason, failed, and was magnified,
As if saying it were a prayer, and a forgiveness.

The students read out passages, their voices
Stumbling, as if speech were an imperfect gift,
Yet there is something they have seen:
That fool Goriot who loved his daughters;
Sara's stubborn will to live completely,
Which means talking, shepherding these young faces
Not toward knowledge maybe, but toward
A freedom ridiculous, failed, even magnificent,
Like that obsessed old man who lost all, gained all.

The Esplanade

I

The ocean churns onto the old slabs
And old iron, as my father and I clamber
Over the esplanade in our jogging sneakers.
A hurricane shattered it when I was a boy,
But now the broken slabs, the color of bread,
And the prongs of wrenched iron, like crawlers
Weeping rust onto the eroded pavement,
Are a zone of permanent ruin along the water's edge.
Weeds thrust from cracks and scratch our legs.
My father's almost eighty years
Have cured him to a lean, silent stiffness.

For years he worked nights, and slept all day
In a stale room at the other end of the house,
His head wedged under the pillows.

I imagine him clutching some gift
Along the tenement streets, when he was a boy,
Working at his father's laundry.
He preserved it in his mind,
A timeless falling world where he still lives;
The gift was for me:
An amazed distance only acrobats could leap.

II

I spent summers here as a boy,
Peering out at the Rockaways,
At the white scooting chips of sailboats.
The bay was windswept, sparkling;
Its emptiness was half inside me.
I lay on a tilted slab, a radio jammed by my ear,
Listening to the love songs of those years:
Heartaches and night sweats were my music then,
As if my mind were a shell where something
Had drunk deep. It was the first of many rooms,
A blur of enclosure: a bedroom rank with adolescent sex,
Another room over Paris rooftops,
A bronze lamp, a clock with a twisted hour hand;

The innocuous matter of days
That took an impression, like soft wax.

This morning we follow the esplanade,
Full of awkward silence, athletic, lean,
Already preparing to jog into the next world.
My father talks in prepared sentences,
Always rehearsing about these waters he has walked
Along every morning for fifty years.
In his constricted voice, almost inaudible,
An exhalation from some crevice in his mind,
He talks about the devil, God's partner
In the human heart. These waves, he says,
May be heaven's heartbeat, but the blood
In our veins is the devil's work.
I too know the devil's work, which brings
Us together here, partners in movement, in failure,
As if he carried me even now in his lean body,
His mind grown sleepy from peering into a dimness.

III

At the far end of the jumbled rock
And cement walk is a chain fence
And a bleak lawn, some unused benches;
The sort of building everyone knows,
A bland skin of squares and angles,
A nest of antennae, empty repeating windows.
As we skirt the fence, my father
Stares at the wintry expanse
Of ocean, grass, the building of tan brick,
With its small orderly windows.
It is a nursing home; my father is an old man.

Sea gulls waddle on the breakwater
Stabbing at bread rinds, or lift off
With powerful thrusts, to skim the incoming waves.
It is a bitter gift: that crashing line of white water,
The meeting of two realms.
My father and I share it now,
Both of us peer into the dimness.

All my life, I have wanted to come closer
To this mild, unforgiving man,
Who exists in my hands and voice,
And is the nervous laughter I hear
Before my throat expels it.

IV

I remember my grandfather's quavering voice,
Sitting beside a window, a few days before he died.
He chanted in Yiddish to his grandson,
Who understood nothing, but stored everything in his memory,
Distended by unsayable fatigue.

An unpainted house, wind singing in the cracks,
The window casting a sheen on the long unused sofa,
The bed with its sad quilt. On the table,
The photograph of a boy with large ears,
A crushed smile, standing beside his father,
Who squints beyond the camera,
A stiff, muscular, beautiful man.

V

Father, there's so much I never asked you,
Now the answers seem trivial.
Yet, for all your angry quiet, your shy nervous body,
What have you saved by living less?

I think of your swallowed angers,
The hurt on your face when I twisted grammar.
All your life, you have wrestled with fears
That would not become angels.
Your crabbed masculinity concealed a motherly
Sweetness you could let out only when you were alone,
With the damp sand at your feet, the foaming waves
Beside you. With an artistry I still marvel at,
You remade yourself in that lonely space,
As you have remade yourself in me.

Stanzas in an Emergency

I

Here is the river,
The salt-tide edging upstream,
Grey cliffs extending in the sunmist.

I will not count my blessings.
I will be blessed.
I will solve the baffled distance in my mind.
I will not panic at my freedom.
I will know the smooth night
When my wife perches beside me,
Plumed and shining, as on a branch.
I will bring the estuary of the grey day
Into everything cramped and scarred.
I will bring you, my puzzled patient friend,
Whom I keep eluding
When you want only to tell me about love.

II

My neighbor emerges
In a clang of tumblers and doors.
With her sad nipples, her daughter vanished into
    permanent winter,
She is stubborn as a nun, and almost beautiful.
I see the news seller on the corner,
His blind face, his daylong
Conversation with dimes and quarters.
I accept my wife's rage, her pride,
The spined flower standing for her in my mind,
The frantic light which is love's exit, or entrance.

III

To exist at the highest level;
To be entirely conscious, so that even my smallest sigh
Glides happily, and the deathwatch is never bored,
For the little one, God's human face,
Death, with his gay elfin whisper,
All the goings-on in closets,
Smothered giggle, lank defeated clothes;
All, all come crowding in, like guests at a wedding,
With promises that only death can keep.

IV

A stubble-faced Greek runs the all-night
Market around the corner.
His bins are full of mangoes, plums,
Crushed sprigs of mint,
Bananas large as clubs, roots for alien stews.
They are colors that play against the night,
Bins of the loveliness that never sleeps.

This Greek in his shop
Stands guard for me, I sleep for him.
Together we endure the night.

Prayer Against Too Much

Late-summer trees;
White flowers thickening around each house,
Where people eat, touch, talk,
Not disturbing the peace they cast
Over the inward and the outward sleep.

An enormous wish:
That nothing be too plentiful;
That grass diminish into lawns,
And the hunt become a ceremony of love.
This harmony is a prayer against too much.

Behind leaf-shadowed windows,
We peer into one well, waiting
For the soft splashing of a stone
Neither of us throws.
At chance points we touch, create shade, drop leaves.
Gradually we have become each other's weather,
As Ovid knew, glimpsing
The soul's destructive music in a face.

The City in the Sea

They come as strangers,
Not yet needing to see, not estranged;
Friends to the air,
To rubbery tugs of the ocean current.
Nor have I known them, except as speech
Comes dripping, inhuman, from the sea.

I accept the furniture of my life:
Green puffed couch and greener rug
Over its quiet acre, Genevieve's toys scattered,
The cat rolled, grey-white, on the chair.

All watch me kindly,
As pieces of the wreck, the puzzle searching to be whole.

Single-Room Occupancy

Last week I walked for hours, and toward midnight
—Broadway was a tunnel of glassy light—
A drunk leaned from a doorway as from
His upright grave, and mumbled,
"How about a quarter?" with his cupped wing
Of a hand, like the disguised messenger
Who came to Abraham out of the dust-wind,
To find if he knew the fluttering,
Helpless light we are.

The Perfect Sleepers

This light flooding my chair
Is too strong at six in the morning;
It was meant for the policemen prowling
In a room around some criminal,
His guilt a form of sleeplessness.

With half-shut eyes, I see horses motionless
in a field
Except for their tails that flick away darkness,
Their eyes blazing like angels
On a beach in hell, bruised but noble,
For they left speech behind them
On their nightlong fall into the world.

Perfect sleepers, erect in the narrow field
Between thinking and dreaming,
Your large eyes merciful, but empty;
I take you with me into the grey milk of dawn,
Knowing your terrors are simpler than mine:
Afraid of puddles, rabbits and the whip,
Not of promises kept or broken, not of breathing,
Not of love's forged signature
And its costly repairs.

The River

I

A bridge over the low-flowing river;
Houses like torn white cards cling to the cliffside.
Ballfields in the park resemble sexual flowers,
The bruised earth of the pitcher's mound,
Foul lines plunging toward the water.

An all-day news broadcast fills my living room,
And the half-life within: enigmas, voices.

For three years, living over this trough
In the earth, I have watched the slow turning
Of the light; years which wrote their scorchings
And frights on me. In its furrow of rock,
Twenty-four stories down, the river was another world,
Vast, clear and sweet, like a bow
Drawn slowly in one never-wavering note.

When my daughter was an hour old, flailing
In the aseptic glow of the hospital cradle,
Her eyes squeezed shut, already bruised by light,
She made thin, rasping sounds,
As if some creature were trapped behind her gums.

Genevieve, one day
You will remember someone: a glimpse,
A voice, telling you what I never told
—What the living never say—
Because the words ran backward in my breath.

II

The other day, with my daughter at the zoo,
The wild stench of the animal house,
Its cackling and screeching, frightened her.
In one cage, a lynx swung back and forth,
Its eyes half closed, feet soundless as a dancer's.

In our century, imprisonment is our romance.
A man looks out his window
With a somber faith resembling hope:
Out there, the forbidden world of sunlight,
The river and the distant hills, hazy and blue,
Like a glimpse of paradise.

My daughter comes halfway up my thigh,
A thin, serious little girl, but already
She has her secrets. Because her face has no past,
She is still only partly human.
Careless and half-bored, she watches the lynx,
And the two of them, blank, curiously elusive,
Make the sidestep that lets time hurtle by.

III

On summer afternoons, the river ignites
With a soft simmering heat,
Dissolving the space of my room,
As if the earth wheeled its smoky globe before my eyes.

Genevieve, can you hear it?
A bird's hoot, or the wheezing throb of a tug?
Nothing is lost; every memory,
The infinite sensations of every day,
Rise up and cover us.

Here is the river. Its honeyed crawl
From nowhere to nowhere, its gun-metal flow,
Will blink as if it had never been.
And the tugboat pushing barges upstream,
The current crumpling at its prow;
Boys in the park playing baseball
On the brown vulva of the ballfield:
That simplicity is not for us, but we love it.

IV

Walking next to me, your hand wrapped
Around my thumb, your capering body
Seems not to touch the ground.

Octagonal paving stones; a fine spray
Of shadows across the Drive;
The iron skeleton of a Junglegym
Where children clamber and slide.
A block down, drummers thump arpeggios
Hollow notes. Beer cans, paper bags.
The dour gait of joggers,
As if life were always uphill, always older.

The river gleams beyond the stone parapet;
It is a nether sky,
A tail drooped indolently in the sun;
A root branching into a continent.

Part Two

A Fly on the Water

I

It is eating me.
It is everything hungry in the world,
And wants me, and I'll tell you, I don't mind.
The women I meet are soft fire;
At night,
Space rattles in my heart;
Your voice,
That muffled angry breathing.

My fathers shuffle the sky; odor of pine trees,
Dark sandy soil. I am lonely,
And think of those sad mystical men in their dark hats,
Who made God's noise when they prayed,
Made it louder in their goose-down beds,
When they clapped their wives' ears
And heard God's drum measuring their bones.

II

A child opens his arms
In the summer heat. With eyes half closed,
He feels the life spilling inside him.
Small and pale on the grass,
He looks almost cruel, he is so happy.

The tree shakes, and God falls out;
Lifetimes of skin and longing stroll naked in the street.
Because it is all I know, I do this;
My text, a joke of the flesh, like eyesight, hummingbirds,
Anything that soars.

III

Stillness spreads from your face
Like ice knitting on a pond.
When it breaks, will God stream past my ankle
Darkly, or as a pool of deadly light?

A fly skates on nothing, on tension:
On something as abstract as a prayer, or as love.

Jacob and the Angel

Like a dried husk, split into a grin,
I stood on the slope of the hill, and listened to
Something rising over the crippled acacia,
The spiky weeds goats grind with their flat yellow teeth.
I could hear them, grunting, half-asleep,
In the glimmering starlight, so bright it could be an edge
Of the final fire, just starting out there.
Something rose over the land; not only darkness trailing
After the sun like a tail, something from me.

I licked dew from these rocks when the wells failed,
Drank goat's blood, and lay with my tongue
Pressed against my teeth. Thirst made me a man,
If a man is someone who drinks pain, and is still thirsty.

And then I was thrown down, as if crumpled
By the lid of the stars. I saw a tree
Rising to heaven, like a brain of thorns;
A wing darting downward, as if a hole
Had plunged earthward and struck me.
My cracked brain of a human being
Bled into the ground,
Half-crazed because God had chosen me.
Why won't He leave me alone, my mouth
Full of dust, my shoulders scorched and breaking?

So Jacob tried to struggle free
Of God's thought, and God's parched burden.

A Theory of Needs

I want what has been sliding
Toward me from the corners of the earth;
What the wind lulls along the early morning streets:
The dancing fit of history,
The fathers, my magnificent liars,
Who tugged until the garment tore,
And the tumbling fall began.

Lovers reaching as I go past,
I am thumb-worn as an old table,
A house askew,
The hole in time made by an old photograph.

All right I'll say it! I betrayed, slept, woke up;
Married, died, exulted.
The bird of sympathy howled in my sleep.

I want to jostle strangers in the street,
No knowing which of them stole death.
Poets made it, philosophers disguised it;
It is mine, a bargain.

Hope

A stalk of yellow weed isolated in sunlight;
The tinge eastward toward Queens over tarred rooftops.

A wake furls slantwise across the empty river,
Cloud-shadows slide over the city.
It is slough time,
Night flows from each little death
Hiding under bright covers, rises, fills all of space.

A room lights up across the street,
And the dusty pane gives the awkward man
Shuffling inside it a softness,
As he walks to the window, walks back,
In the wakefulness of his white room,
Its ruffled paper globe over the light bulb,
Alive in no one's eyes.

It comes, you are moving toward it,
You will be alive until you die.
The sadness in people's faces won't be for you.
It will be like weather,
A tattoo of light through gaps in the clouds,
The juttings of light, the splinterings, the wonderings.

The children cough in their sleep,
An indigo sky looms over black walls.
Drip, drip goes the gathered knob of night.
You are contained in your portion of endlessness,
Pregnant as white porcelain.
Catch me, you say, oh, catch me!

The Other Side

When I was a boy, I remember asking my father if the quantity of stars in the night sky was written down anywhere. Since the number existed, I argued, it had to exist somewhere. I think I imagined a rug folded back, with something written in the corner. It was the side of things your feet never walked on; the pool of all the thoughts you never had, and the faces you never saw.

The mystery of that other side was its clarity, which I recognized years later, when I read about heavens full of thrones and spheres, and divine musicmakers churning on the rim of each sphere; depths in the mind inhabited, unbeknownst to us, by personalities sending light-waves to the surface where they shine mysteriously as ourselves, but are really a sort of code expressing the layer of life inside us, where everything is clear.

Sometimes, you don't know how, your mind gets around to that other side. You see the number in the corner, and write it down. You see, and become personally acquainted with love, pain, death, your own body. Because of these skids to the other side, the abstractions I have mentioned tend to have a personal warmth for you. A dust of clarity clings to them, enabling them, mere words though they be, to throb, smile, gnash their teeth, even kill.

Birth

What? That spurt of sudden green,
Happy in thin sunlight
This cold April on Broadway;
The café's fogged window,
The half-seen faces, open-lipped, budding.
Their seeds roost in the dark of eyes,
The spiral passages of ears.
Come out with me!
Let's gather the flimsy stars of the words of others,
Falling God knows how, God knows where.

The Art of Sacrifice

Our breath on the altar is offered in love.
The fuck-you we smile is offered in love.

The faucet bubbling with anxiety
And the mirror fishing for loneliness,

The worm we cut into lengths and serve,
Calling it day by day, are offered in love.

So much love, and I am hiding,
Exploring inside the wall, pretending no one is there.

Terror

A circle traced by a finger
I must live within.

What strange fulfillment!
The psalmist plucks handfuls of bright nails.

Chill sober love,
Sole bather on this beach without echoes,

You feel the bunched waters
Sliding in milky disorder at your feet.

Waiting for the Storm

Will I know him in heavy sunlight,
Waiting for the storm?

Will he come dribbling a scuffed ball,
In and out of shadows,

Feinting, laughing to his friends?
Or will he balance on white wings,

A creature of water, of air?
I wait, I look.

If you were crystal, this voice
Would be your nerves.

The numbers on my watch
Are your stutter-step.

There is a property of June;
It is almost blue.

Tomorrow we will call it time.
We will be lying.

Losing Track

I think of your worried face,
Your love spinning its orbit of planetary woe.

A headlight pivots across the wall; our bed
Expanding to a thin line where sky and water meet.

Am I a man, a woman? Am I you, myself?
It is time to forget what I know.

I love you, and climb down
To drink at the opaque river, bathe,

Feel the blunt blows of fish
Against my skin,

And for a moment, lose my confused panic
At life's hunger that feeds on me.

Lightning Flashes over the Palisades

The crooked seams of oncoming night;
My breakable body; its prayer
To the grey pearly assault, in this country
Of new time, the time that ends,
A gulping embrace, part water, part air.

A wild pucker suddenly churns the river,
The white needle jerking silently up and down.

One Summer Before Man

Listen! The undergarments of the women
Are rustling OM. It is the Sanskrit
Of skin, the Hebrew of hair.
I have made a breath-tunnel in the air,
And now I plant my kiss upon you,
Naked as a woman in the blue neon of love,
Or as the looping antennae strung over
Miles of the desert in Arizona, which listen
To the spaces between stars, and hear heavy breathing;
Or else as the noiseless snipping
Of surgical scissors as they part the living tissue,
Bringing to light that which had been dark.

So much was known that will not be known.
The ways of the animals; some angles
Of sunlight on a blue window;
Or what the cow-mother said at the crossing
Of the paths, one summer before man,
When nothing had received a name,
And silence had not yet acquired
Its present unutterable scandal
(The scandal of crushed almonds, or of ozone;
Or of industrial processes accomplished by no human hand),
Before even beauty and its needlework,
Which is all that we remember.

Gather close, children, I will tell you
About that bellowing on the hill.
It is the cow-mother whose words
We have stolen for our purpose
(Here is the sack where the severed words lay).
She has no tongue, she bleats at the piss-yellow
Moon, a wheezing asthmatic sigh.
And then, swallowing all the summer's wild grass,
The blackberries, the succulent plants
Spreading their labia under the oak trees;
Swallowing the turds of small animals,
And the clattering of the dragonflies,
Those Japanese warriors, she swells, she swells!
And then, oh, children, from her mouth
Which knows no future because it is toothless,
Backward, and tight as a sphincter,
From her musical anus, she sings.

Anything Long and Thin

All traffickings upward out of the earth
Or sideways across it: longitudes,
Desperations; the glue of sentences
(Their meanings bunched and dense,
A glare of light, a space seizing
You with coarse hands).
Anything long and thin, the idea of poverty,
Love wrested into a question mark
Like a man violently breathing out.
And the train trips, the trajectories of airplanes,
A knife slitting the infinite until it touches home,
And the life stumbles on its imaginary
Thread over the abyss. Ship wakes, rivers,
The shy proddings of the grass.
And then, more tender than eyesight:
Eternity mooning in a glass,
Or a flagpole stubbing itself against the sky.
And everything that won't stay still:
Your swinging hair, your voice reminding me
That God is a freeze-frame in my heart,
Or a flickering in my lymph; or maybe
A silence this evening, looking down
At the barges with their white wakes,
The sea gulls wheeling over the water.
Time flattened by a goldbeater's hammer
Becomes space: buds, twigs, shy leaves,
And a fistful of roots, *chiendent*.
They say we are renewed every seven years,
Except for the scars of past weariness
The Hindus call samskaras.
Only they live on, as a net of furrows on our brain,
The small lightnings that dim our eye.

Breaking

Scissors; the farting of outboard
Motors; the muscular stranglings
Of the foul wind that blows from whatever empty well,
From whatever gateway into the garden from the
    clanging house,
From whatever lung-pit dug into cold hills,
And now emitting breakages and pearls, figurines and turds;
All those remnants, all those shards;
While the unbroken wind coils
Around the earth grasping its tail.
Earthworms part, hardly noticing that they are two.
Seeds break from the mother tree;
Lovers go about with their wounded stumps;
I turn from you and see the incredible chill of space.
Patience! The paramecium will inherit the earth.
A face will pass by in that swarming
Solitude which is the soul's light.

Bless the Earth, Bless the Fire

Here is the wanderer with
His unwrapped soul, his parcels of pure voice.
Oh, cloud of unravelings,
Root hairs of the saints descending
Into the sorcerer's night with obsidian tools
Of silence, to root out the unspoken ones,
Food for the thought which is never thought.

Take a flint egg, hatch it.
Take a mouth that hasn't spoken for a thousand years,
A mouth of night, mouth of Simeon Stylites
When the devil made his tongue into a bird's penis.
Take a handful of syllogisms, eat them.
Sit with the patience of gasoline,
Until after the last bomb has consumed its name;
And then, in a voice that is an hourglass,
A voice of the scissorings of time,
Bless the earth, bless the fire.

This You May Keep

A showering of branches,
Leaves in all their fits, their sultry shakes,
Like voices circling in a room,
Uninvited, but hovering, whirling,
An undulant map.

Surrender first your words:
On crisp stems, without pain or hope,
They defy all sense, all green.

Give up the future next:
There can be no waiting;
Even sloth is an urgent leafy crawl.

And the gaunt motorcyclist;
The old-fashioned mirror with no backing,
Only a tattered scar where your face is;
And the queen of dusty rooms,
The lady of hopes, give her up too.

This you may keep.
A smell of rain from the pavement,
This day of heat and mist.
And the leaves, their heavy silence;
Not even the hope of a way;
Only flesh in its looseness, its transactions with light,
Its whispering underfoot,
Its berries, some edible, some bitter.

Life Story

I

I speak, and don't want to lie.
How my past gives off a lean light;
Everywhere strangers inviting me, frightening me,
As if they were mysteries from God;
And I the only human being on earth.

I speak of sunlight on the roof-edge,
Listening to Mozart, a Vedic chant:
Twigs crackling in a fire;
While my wife shines in her mysterious rage.

II

If there is an Eden, it isn't past,
But coming: a beach in autumn;
A man trekking silently on the sand
While the sunlight rains down.
The stages of life pass by; the beach swelling
Its pale sprout, until it bursts
In showers of pain and light:
The fright of death, of growing old.

III

A boy with splayed ears,
A slack look on his face.
When I wake anxiously during the night,
A wall touches my eyelids
And I know he's on the other side,
Near a basement furnace,
A coal pile sparkling in the fire-glimmer.

I watch him push the cellar door
And feel his way downstairs,
While sweet summer air mingles
With musty coal, dark with dark.

His father and mother wheel among the galaxies;
He is the night's child. Not the dark's,
The child of space, of the low rumble
Shaking the air, like the god in the story
Slumbering fitfully under everything.

IV

The creak of an old floor;
A battered velvet couch, with her shape
Still hollowed in it;
A drunken swaying in the middle of the room,
Where our voices swerve and fall
Against a far wall.

Talking to her now,
Hearing her wake to a life she does not love;
Reading my life in her changed body,
While our daughter peers
Over the railing of her crib, frighteningly curious,
As if everything fit from beginning to end.
That's how the story begins.

Part Three

The House

I

It has walls of the flat, breakable rock
Farmers still plough out of neighboring fields,
Roof beams of twisted oak,
Mortar of red clay, grooved deeply on the west
Where storms come in from the Atlantic
Over these once flooded hills.

It was built by a farmer's youngest son
Who took what was left, a few southward-
Tilted acres, chestnut woods, a pond.
This was wine country then;
The steep rocky slopes were good for that.
Along the hill crest, beside the old coach road,
Houses shepherded their vines.
Now, scrub oak and chestnut, lean spiked acacia.

The beautiful indifference of this land!
The brittle weeds in fields still half ploughed
From when he climbed into his bed, and never left it.
They say he was a short, likable man.
Who carved mystic runes on the doorpost,
And ploughed with a team of oxen,
Their horns sheathed in tin, harness
Of black oiled leather. I found the old yoke,
Dark with sweat, and polished it, hung it up,
To remind me that others had lived here
Before me; what I loved was their labor,
Elastic, hard as singing wire.

II

You don't build a stone house,
You coax it from the earth, like a bud
Perched on the mother-branch, and hugging it:
Walls a yard thick,
Windows narrow as *meurtrières*,
Roof tiles that gong when you strike them.

And a stone house doesn't change,
Like a farmer, thin and tanned
In his measureless old age.
Pacing his fields, his slowly ripening woods
Of oak and chestnut, death means nothing to him.

III

That first autumn I turned the garden with a pick and hoe,
Hammered an edge onto my scythe as my neighbor taught me;
I swam on the black earth, eating its glossy meat.
I heard no one, saw nothing.

My young wife listened to the radio
And grew thin. She became a silence.
Who could she talk to? Who could she dream of, and touch?
That fall the fireplace was her lover,
Her evenings licked into a phantom of fire.
At night, on the ridge,
She hooted at the oak fringe
Beyond the field. An owl's bell-like answer
Came, cautious and probing.
The moon pressed on the tiles of the house,
A ladder of clouds lowering the sky.

IV

That year something full of bitterness
And wild attention lived through me.
I watched the grape vines darken,
Their green fruit swelled, burst,
The rough cable of their trunks sagged to the ground.
Lizards ran in swift stabs over the gravel.
A walnut tree cast looping branches into the wind
That blew here when there were nothing
But forests, hermits, and devils tormenting them.

My wife and I slept in an oak bed, in the room
We had whitewashed, a single window,
Twisted irregular beams.
She hated the wildness, but even our bed
Where she took refuge, a square of soft clean linen,
Couldn't keep it from her.
Alone in that whiteness,
Listening to her deepest wish answering it angrily,
She became hard and pale.

v

When spring came, I planted dahlias
In a cleared patch near the house,
Gangly plants with heavy leaves
And thick bent heads that unclasped,
Red, purple, white.
They grew taller; stalks and flowers.
With their curved necks, they resembled
Unsmiling girls, their colors
Like a breath not fully breathed.

They were beautiful invalids, and I nursed them.
Crab grass and wild clover tried to choke them.
The ground hardened, the sun was heavy.
I carried pond water to them every evening,
Pulled the weeds up around their tough pink roots.
In the morning, I watched the flowers flare
And catch the early light.
By August, the tallest was as tall as I was.

How curiously human they looked,
How empty the house was.
My wife sat cross-legged on the oak bed.
Her door stood open to her enemy, the sun,
And her other enemy,
For by then I had become that.

VI

By now we couldn't see each other.
I was lonely, but couldn't say it;
We had become each other's negative,
Her body hardened by isolation,
And I, pleasureless, tough with need,
Wanting to be as motionless as the sun,
Predictable, walking with the heavy tread
Of the old men who had survived death,
And were now totems of brooding skin,
Leaning on two canes or
Straight as weeds on a hilltop.

How can I explain myself?
Here was refuge,
Here was the place I'd recognized,
Where I'd come to be saved from the fright of living;
These few acres cleared by people
I never knew, two stone rooms, floorless,
Cows breathing next to them,
The rafters creaking with the weight of harvest,
Wild fodder grass in the attic,
Tobacco hung in yellow sheathes
From the roof beams.
Time moved mutely in the leaves
Changing day by day,
In the yellowing lilacs, in the labored breath
Of the white sky blowing hot and long every day.

I can explain only myself,
But not the coldness that settled
Between us like a person,
The house thick with avoidance,
The lovelessness, the feeling that nothing
In the world existed but her expressionless face.

She was young, she had followed me here.
Now, after a year in this stone house,
A year of the rasping wind which blew
Before time began, and still makes its mockery
Of speech, which they heard in caves twenty thousand
Years ago, and witches heard in their dens
Of chestnut trees, and farmers on those stormy nights,
When the crops were at stake,
And I hear like a disorder in my mind,
There is nothing left between us
But our failure to understand.

The Question

Stone-blue winter;
The upswept brush of winter oak
Vibrates in the wind, expectant, bridelike.

Who am I?
An insect, startled, still sleeping
By the fire.

A bird clings to the telephone wire
Behind the house; an exultant questioning
Booms at its feet. When we die,
We hug the living to us as we never did;
We notice their creased skin, their quick eyes
That slide away, seeing more than they intended.

Who is that moving beside you,
So at ease, so colorless?
What can that dark flutter
Of his say to you, his voice thinned
To pass death's membrane?

Wasps

This morning I thumbed the spray-can,
And they stumbled from the rafters,
From the cheap rippled glass of the kitchen pane,
Until a striped carpet jerked over the tiles,
Or lay curled and still, like pebbles of bruised velvet.

When I cautiously churned a stick
Into their grey nest, papery, almost a mist,
The chaff of wing-wisps fluttered to the floor.
Now squads of ants tow them away.

A tractor's frayed howl rises from the valley.
Otherwise it is quiet, baked dust, marigolds.
Yet those heavy-bellied wasps stumbling over the tiles
Stay with me: their inaudible rage whines in my ear.
Listen to them in the pale stubble,
In the wild flowers, like small stings of color,
Poppy-red, cornflower blue.
My own breathing frightens me,
The precarious daylight hollowed by their knife-like wings.

Early Waking

Again the ashen light,
A tiny spider swinging on its pendulum thread
Against the pane.

Lately, I don't sleep much.
It's not anxiety, but a curious feeling
That I must pay attention, or death will gain on me.

A brightening across the valley,
Individual stalks of grass concentrate the light.
The red glossy leaves of the wild plum tree behind the house,
And the faded green nuggets of the young walnuts.
A cloud leans across the sky;
A faintly gusting wind in the oaks
And juniper, as if to say:
Nothing stops or begins, this whispering is all,
This tender faded light is all.

Parting the Sea

Fog hides the shallow ditch, no more
Than a grassy furrow, marking the edge of our land.
Oak trees and thorned acacia bend over it,
Like combers of a green sea.
The thinning out begins on this side,
Where there is barley, tobacco,
Green peas climbing on a spindly branch.
So much naming is not natural.
It must be cared for, thinned
And watered every day.
Listen!
The cruelty of trees, burst rivers
Of oak and fern, lap crazily around it.

To farm you need a sharp edge,
Something that doesn't know you're there;
You need to give up owning
This patch-sized farm on the earth's outer rim.

Remember the human body was trimmed
From something bigger and worse:
Identity sobs in the branches of trees,
Shouts from the stubble of the mown fields.
Either you have no enemies, or only enemies.

And Yet…

It's true, we carry the world inside us,
Always present like light.
And yet, this hilltop where the sun sits,
Heavy and red, every evening;
My house shuttered now, the gravel courtyard
Sprouting weeds; myself, woefully transient,
My suitcase packed, listening for
My neighbor who will take me to the train,
And the stillnesses mobbing past,
Strangely clamorous and thick.
It's true, I know. And yet, and yet!

The Other Ocean

1974

It was the whip-marks of the horned asp,
And the Beduin sucking his coffee
Through cracked fleshy lips;
It was his ceremonial kindness
In the month-long solitude of camel-watching,
While his animals bellowed over the plain
Like ghosts roaming in the star-glitter.
It was these scattered lives in a country without rain,
And the miniature within,
Crawling, hissing,
Its light almost solid, almost mineral.

The way back smelled of cinders,
Older, emptier than anything living;
A way of faces lost in the changes
Of light into dark, passing grief-wrinkled
Boulders, sand glaring red and grey.

It was a line of rust scrawled on the stillness,
As a sown darkness, and an expectation.

The Taking Away

The close-fitting sleepless night,
Everything still: the woodchuck in its hole
Under the rock pile, the apple tree outside my window.
In the aftermath of rain, a taking away:
Color, shape, sound, as if the darkness
Had flowed from my own eyes,
Dropping slow black flakes over the ground.

On nights like this, I think
Of a companion waiting in my armchair
For the first milk of dawn.
Not knowing his face, I say he looks like me.
I say we fit one shadow, and that he once
Was grateful to the moon for following
Everywhere over the earth,
Even on that mineral night when everything
Human failed me, and I knew it would be years
Before I was whole enough to be a father,
Or a friend.

Now I lie awake in my New England brass bed,
Listening for lulls in the wind, when
The miles of birch and oak,
Patches of the fields between, breathe in;
And for a moment it is my breath,
My midsummer dark, veined with cold currents.
I am happy to lie in its shade,
To savor its fruit, and admire
Its icy grains sprouting down the night.

Eternity's Woods

I

I have come to this house
Of soft angular stone, wondering
How much must fall away before I have nothing.

Here is the raw path
That the Romans slashed across these hills,
And pilgrims trudged into crumbling rock;
Now it is an old scar, smelling of wild mint,
Rosemary, tiny wild orchids under the blackberry brambles.

The old farmer who built this place
On five acres of stiff red soil,
Good only for barley and a bitter wine,
Never saw a Jew in his life;
Yet I imagine him beside me,
His head tilted thoughtfully,
While a woodpecker jeers in the horse-chestnut tree.

II

I bought the house a dozen years ago.
For its calcareous stone, its oak beams so tough
They bend your nails. Even when there were vines,
And bitter grapes hung to the ground,
Only a poor farmer could have loved it.

Today his grandson, Jean, lives in the valley
Although he still comes up here when he can, to breathe freely
And tell me about the forest his grandfather knew;
The witches who cooked souls in open pots,
The quilted silence of the chestnut woods,
Where even brambles couldn't grow,
Only mushrooms that came and went, like odorous ghosts.

A hard red road scrapes the bones of the hill.
The parched field boils with cicadas;
A delirium of white scraps wobbling in the air,
Butterflies, the dance of life.

All my running has ended here:
The baked fragrant summer air,
The postman's yellow van coming to a halt,
The envelopes with their white chill of distance.

A shimmer of heat distorts eternity's woods,
And the butterflies wink over the field,
Half-wild, half-cruel,
Like the laughter of a solitary man.

III

There are times when you have nothing, are nothing:
A beach in cold October air
Breathing the space that held you;
Or a coal-dark basement, naked,
The night breeze garlanding your bare skin.

Now I have come to these clay-mortared rocks,
This walnut tree unraveling its shade
On the coarse gravel. Lying
On a manger ledge, in the bedroom, a stable once,
While iced fields of the Milky Way look on,
I wake in thick dark, unable to name my fright,
Until day drips, greys, and I come out into the leaf-gleams,
Alive in the bite of morning.

The End Circulates in the Wide Space of Summer

I

We hardly speak.
You have been here so long
You are like another leg or arm.
We trot across the ice,
Approach the book, and enter it.
You read the text,
I try to hear what you are saying.

The sky shivers,
A bird moves across it like a flexible blade.

So it began.

II

The end circulated in the wide space of summer,
With sawing of small insects, bubbles
Clustering in ponds.

I try to hear what you are telling me,
But the smile of an invisible cat consumes the sky;
That singsong call of young girls
Jumping rope is death's nursery rhyme.

III

Where in this endless room
Is the one who loves me,
The hissing of her silks?

We talk of God, his mica angels,
His book of living wormed in rock.
We have what lasts,
And the soft perishable mind, which doesn't.
We have the spacious word
Where nothing begins, and goes on beginning,
As long as we live.

Postscript
by Galway Kinnell

When writing prose, Paul Zweig was an astonishingly swift and articulate writer. But his poetry, which he wanted to write most of all, came with great difficulty. If the pressure to "let it out," as Walt Whitman called it, leads one to write, this pressure must have built up in the first place because of something that inhibits expression of intimate feelings and makes writing difficult. Something like this may have been behind Paul's struggle with poetry.

From the time I met Paul Zweig in Paris in 1960 and until his death in the summer of 1984, I saw him slowly learn to write freely: to break down his inhibitions against intimate self-revelation, and to let himself flow into other things and other lives according to the riddle, "I was the man, I suffered, I was there." In *Eternity's Woods,* these poems of his late forties, after twenty-five years of struggle, he wonderfully succeeds.

And he kept on going. Last summer, under the strictures of time brought up short, Paul wrote at incredible speed, mostly on a book on pre-history and on his autobiography, but, also, at unexpected moments, on poetry. "I'm just letting the poems pour out," he wrote, "I don't know what they say or mean." He had gone beyond the self-conscious efforts of one who sits down at a desk with sharpened pencil and sheets of white paper to "write a poem." He turned his back on poetry, and found all around him the subjects of poetry; and poems burst from him. What he wrote in those inspired last months affirms that his life as a poet was coming to full flower.

After James Wright's death I remarked to Annie Wright on how cruel it was that Jim died just as he had come into his full powers as a poet. Annie replied: "Yes, I feel that, too. But if he had to die, isn't it much better this way? Would we have wanted him to die empty and exhausted?" And I also can see that the knowledge of death is part of the essence of these last poems —it shines in their freedom, their intensity, the idolatrous attachments.

All the poems of Paul's final summer, rough as they are, must be published one day as a chapbook. But admirers of *Eternity's Woods,* I know, will want to have a glimpse of them now. Here is a poem—untitled—and a part of a poem.

Poem

I don't know if I can bear this suddenly
Speeded up time. I pull the blinds
And it is morning. White flowers gleam
Under the linden leaves. The cathedral's red dome
Dwarfs the timid skyline across the river,
A town like any other: Cars grinding
Over the cobbles, the perishable mosaic of fruits
And vegetables in front of small stores.
The dead look on indifferently from their green horses,
From their pedestals where they receive the homage of pigeons.
There are no old men here, only quick boys,
And girls dancing out of their clothes.
The old men loiter in the museums
Nursing their small immortalities.
Can you smell it? The car fumes, coffee, breath,
Old leather, urine, a young woman's perfume.
It smells of youth, death, sleepless nights;
It never looks up, doesn't see
The blank enduring looks of the statues;
And yet it is a kind of poem.
But now I'm thinking of those green men
Concentrated in their single, undistracted movement,
Their heads pulled belligerently back
While they tug on the reins of a bronze horse,
Their eyes like termites boring holes in nothing,
Because they have hit on the one gesture
That will never fail of completion;
Their whole perishable selves squeezed into
A green eroded look that chuckles at the stupidities
Of springtime and young girls, from their own springtime
Of ominous, wretched, sour verdure.
Oh, the egotists, the zany gods commemorating
One or another of the lies men tell

To garnish their forgettable lives: the legends,
The Bibles; the enormous whisper rising like a cloud of bees,
A shimmer of golden motes, and their honey!
Fluid as water, transparent, sweet,
So that anyone who tastes it forgets father and mother,
Lover, children, money, cancer, failed hopes.
Oh, the cunning, amazing story turning the fear of life
Into the love of life. The statues
Enjoy the joke, although they don't laugh,
Or even smile; while the girls gather their
Hair, and the boys call out
Mysterious passwords of blood and sperm, and a sweet smell
Comes from the fruit-stands, where cherries,
Apricots, peaches, plums soften and sag;
A cloying liquid wets the tilted boxes,
Darkening the sidewalk. Soon it will be evening.

Fragment

"*Ca y'est, cette fois.*" This is it, I know it.
To know it all deeply; to have it press up
Like earth-blood out of the crooked old peach tree
In front of the house, propped up on sticks,
But nursing its peaches year after year
Until it seems to hunch lower and want to lie down,
And the peaches swell with long-cooked sweetness,
Orange, yellow and pink.
To know the greying green of late summer
Like a happiness on the earth, a ripening
Into heat and dryness, plums, chestnuts, leeks,
Into tobacco and walnuts
And the evil-smelling pigs that resemble trapped men
In their rooted up squares of yard full of stumps and furrows,
All to make it happy, that creature of fat, flesh
And delicious blood, every ounce of whom
Will be cut up, bled off, ground up,
Until only a few bones will end up feeding the dogs.
Its guts stuffed full of cooked blood
Will hang in the attic; its hams, packed
In a chest of salt, will stew all winter;
Its flesh, salted and ground with juice of truffle,

Will cook in jars and be saved.
To know every inch of it; every wind sliding
From the west full of wet ocean air;
Every pinched odor of the paper-mill ten miles north,
The distant grumble of the machines
That augur of good weather, north weather.
And every variety of silence, the vocabulary
Of it not in our language: the cicadas on hot afternoons,
Pine worms creaking in the rafters;
The leanings of white barley, and the hum
Of small winds on the ear, almost an internal sound,
A blood sound; the silence before
The dawn colors begin and the blue silence of the last light
With a couple of large stars;
Layerings of it, full of speech
And smells, and of all except the human voice.
To know it year after year: To know the slide
into winter, the last feeble pushings of fodder grass
Not worth harvesting, unless you turn the cows loose in it,
And watch the brown turds form like flowers
On the yellow ground.
The hunters stumbling past apologetically;
The hollow roar of their shotguns;
A couple of deer bounding across my field one morning,
And behind them the baying of dogs,
A crew of mongrels with pink, daffy tongues.
Long afterward the hunters arrive, their guns slung under their arms,
More interested in the bottle in their bag
Than in the deer who are probably over the next hill
By now, trembling knee-deep in leaves.
To know so much: to take these five acres
Of fruit trees, these puny fields, the house built with flat stones
Ploughed out of the ground, and cemented with
Red clay, its roof of crooked oak beams
And tiles so old they sing in the rain;
To spy the cretaceous fossil shells that speak
Of ancient seas, and the shining flints
That speak of men, and know I am here,
And have been here; that time has spread its wares;
That every stone has its story,

Every wind speaks its mind, and there is
A birth-giving, a bringing-forth of days
That is not time, but space; memory;
The irrecoverable home.

OTHER BOOKS BY PAUL ZWEIG

POETRY
Against Emptiness
The Dark Side of the Earth

PROSE AND CRITICISM
The Heresy of Self Love
Lautréamont: The Violent Narcissus
The Adventurer
Walt Whitman: The Making of the Poet

AUTOBIOGRAPHY
Three Journeys: An Automythology

ABOUT THE BOOK

Eternity's Woods has been composed in Sabon by Marathon Typography Service of Durham, North Carolina. It was printed on 70 lb. Mohawk Superfine Softwhite Smooth and bound by Contemporary Lithographers of Raleigh, North Carolina. Design is by Joyce Kachergis Book Design and Production, Inc. of Bynum, North Carolina. Photographs are by John Theilgard.